JUST BREATHE

# JUST BREATHE

A Modern-Day Exodus Journey
to Revive Your

## SOUL

# JUST BREATHE

## A Modern-Day Exodus Journey to Revive Your SOUL

Andrea P.
### BOURGEOIS

Arabelle Publishing, LLC
Chesterfield, VA

PUBLISHED BY ARABELLE PUBLISHING
PO Box 2841
Chesterfield, VA 23832

Unless otherwise noted, scripture quotations are from
The Holy Bible, New International Version ©  1973, 1984
by International Bible Society,
used by permission of Zondervan Publishing House.

Credits:
Foreword written by Amanda Florczykowski
Cover and Interior Design Julie Basinski

Library of Congress Control Number: 2020951924
Subjects Religion / Bible Studies / General
Paperback ISBN 9781735632803

Printed in the United States of America
2021

Group Sales:
Books are available in special quantity discounts when purchased directly from the publisher in bulk by corporations, organizations, and special interest groups. For more information, please email the publisher at
hello@arabellepublishing.com

DEDICATED TO
Y HUSBAND, BRIAN AND OUR SON, PAYNE

JUST BREATHE

# PRAISE FOR JUST BREATHE

Jesus Christ is the same yesterday, today, and forever. (Hebrews 13:8) It is us, in our humanity, who have hills and valleys, who move toward and away from God.

This Bible study came out at a time in my life where I was stagnant. I knew God. I knew of His love. I was going to church and following the commandments; however, I had no spark. There was little joy in my heart and I was spiritually dry. From day one in 'Just Breathe' I was wrecked. The song 'Here's My Heart' by Lauren Daigle captivated me. This study helped me acknowledge and become more aware of where I was and also where I wanted to be, on a journey of forgiveness, restoration, and believing in God's promises. This study took me from a place of stagnation and I began the journey to full surrender and whole hearted trust!!

*-Megan B. Ethridge*

The Bible study completely brought me back to the beginning of my journey with Christ and made me rethink each step of my walk with Him. What I did to go against Him and His will for my life, and times that I didn't think I was worthy of His love, healing, or miracles. This Bible study helped to strengthen my faith in God and really helped me to find peace with God in the fact that He has the answer to all of my questions and concerns. I finally realized that He does show me scripture for everything if I just take the time to talk with Him and read His word! He has shown me scripture after scripture in affirmation of my recent prayers. Lastly, I learned that journaling my prayers really helps when sharing my walk with Christ to others just as we journaled throughout this Bible study.

*-Taylor W. Lafleur*

## WEEK 1: REFLECT - JOURNALING

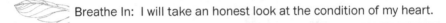 Breathe In: I will take an honest look at the condition of my heart.

Day 1 - Where Am I with God?
Day 2 - Am I Growing Closer?
Day 3 - What Causes Me to Doubt God?
Day 4 - Have I Felt His Presence?
Day 5 - Do I Believe He is Who He Says He is?

## WEEK 2: RINSE - COMING OUT OF EGYPT

Breathe In: I will reflect on what being washed in the blood of Jesus truly means and grasp why He sends a helper.

Day 6 - Egypt
Day 7 - The Red Sea
Day 8 - His Grace
Day 9 - The Veil Was Torn - He Sends a Helper
Day 10 - Spiritual Fullness in Christ

## WEEK 3: RESTORE - FORGIVENESS & HEALING

Breathe In: I will lay down my burdens at the feet of Jesus, will forgive those who have trespassed against me, and will forgive myself for my failures and bad choices.

Day 11 - Forgiveness Is a Choice
Day 12 - My Past
Day 13 - He Qualifies the Called
Day 14 - My Purpose
Day 15 - Restoring and Reflecting

# WEEK 4: REAP - HUNGER FOR MORE IN THE WILDERNESS

Breathe In: I will recognize The Lord as my Shepherd, will commit to His ways, and will witness His provision and faithfulness.

Day 16 - Armor of God
Day 17 - Back to the Basics
Day 18 - Prayer:  Be Real. Be Open.
Day 19 - Manna and Quail. Pillar by Night and Cloud by Day
Day 20 - Taste and See the Lord is Good

# WEEK 5: REVIVE - JEHOVAH JIREH IGNITES A FIRE

Breathe In:  I will cross over into the Jordan River with God and learn what it means to step out in faith and trust Him fully.

Day 21 - His Plans Are Bigger
Day 22 - Crossing Over
Day 23 - Walk on Water with Jesus and Stand on the Promises of God
Day 24 - Discernment
Day 25 - Follow Jesus because He is Faithful

# FORWARD

## by Amanda Florczukowski

## WELL, OF COURSE, I'D BE HAPPY TO!

Andrea matched my excited in a haphazard inquiry to take a picture of my friend and me at a leadership and writing conference ages ago. Our first introduction was in that atrium when I freely sought the closest available "photographer". In her sweet, southern drawl, she invited my friend and me into conversation and surprisingly made us both feel like we had known her forever despite being strangers.

This would come to be the mark of Andrea's personality. She invites people in; through relationship, through words, through actions, and story. She is one the most magnanimous examples of the pure heart God has for people.

As our stranger status has moved into friendship, I have seen Andrea only continue to take her leadership and abilities and use it for others' good. So, when I heard she was finally putting on paper the burning passion she's had for years, I was thrilled to be first in line to take in her words of wisdom. I knew we would all be blessed by her message.

Her message is a unique one -- a message you wouldn't know existed behind her sparkling eyes and joyful countenance; pain. But Andrea has taken the troubles of life and seen them through a perspective not many do. Andrea sees purpose in all things and by God's glory. She sees trials, like the beautiful story from generations past, the Israelite enslavement that moved into the glory of promise, as a backdrop of her life's mantra. We get out of the way. God moves in. He is trustworthy. Even when our feelings and emotions scream that life is unbearable, we mentally shift our perspective to know, when we don't feel, His goodness.

Andrea calls us to acknowledge our own shortcomings as purposeful, an opportunity to see God's ability to fulfill the cracks of those personal insufficiencies and deficits we all experience on this side of heaven. She is an action taker who calls us to risk. She doesn't want anyone to live in the mediocrity of their faith. But, not from a perspective of negativity and "don'ts." Instead, Andrea offers in these pages the benefits of believing and the rewards of obedience in all their glittering glory. She points to why it is vital to live in the fullness of the Believer's life in Christ and why everything else falls short using vivid imagery and deep personal reflection.

We are called to win this race that God has drawn each of us to run. Imagine running with all your might, sweat falling down your forehead as the sun hits your now sensitive skin. Sore from the first half of the run, but hopeful you are half-way there, you want to persevere. You push past your exhaustion and take in deep, hearty breaths that fill your lungs with fresh air that quickly turns into hope. You can do this. You are doing this. Then, in a moment's split-decision, you simply decide to walk off the course and sit on the sidelines. You excuse yourself from the glorious opportunity to win. Believer, you were meant to keep going. Andrea hands you the baton and cheers you on as your biggest fan. What a gift to have this book in your hands, to keep running the race and finish well.

AMANDA FLORCZYKOWSKI
*Author of Bestseller Unraveled:*
*Mothering Fiercely In a World Full of Fears*
Founder of Vigilant Families anti-child trafficking
training and Able Moms International

# THANK YOU

I have to start by THANKING my husband, Brian. From encouragement and support to keeping our little monkey out of my hair so I could write and make edits, I couldn't have done without you by my side! I love you.

I want to THANK my parents and my in-laws for keeping their grandson busy and entertained as I wrote, made edits, and filmed the videos, etc. Y'all are my biggest supporters and have been such an enormous help!

THANK YOU, Jordan Sellers for all the marketing and consulting work throughout this writing journey and filming and producing all the videos for this study. Thank you for believing in me and seeing potential when I couldn't. Thank you for helping me get noticed in the publishing world! You helped me arrive!

A huge THANK YOU to Arabelle Publishing for giving me this opportunity for my first publication. Thank you for taking your chance on me and believing in my work. Thank you for making this experience and process so enjoyable and exciting.

I want to THANK my intern, Morgan Wainwright and my co-worker, Cassidy Collins for all your help designing graphics and merch as well as collaborating and executing my first book launch! I loved working with you on these projects.

I WANT TO GIVE SPECIAL THANKS to these women. They have been strategically placed in my life by our Heavenly Father to encourage me along in this writing journey. The ladies at Table 44, my Marco gals, my sister, and the ladies in our October Bible study. I couldn't have gotten this far without you! THANK YOU for loving me, encouraging me, and standing by my side.

THANK YOU to my Prayer Team from First Moss Bluff Church and FaithWalk ladies praying for me since the summer of 2019 as I took my first leap of faith to become a published author. Martha, Cheryl, Mona, Debby, Robbie, Brandi, Samantha, Alicia, Miranda, and Donna. Donna also a special thank you for using this Bible study with your women's ministry at you and your husband's church.

THANK YOU, Megan and Kara for doing the study as part of your quiet time and sharing with me how it truly revived your soul and set you on a new journey with the Lord. And for all your help in the book launch, as well!

THANK YOU to my friends who did this study with me when it was still a google doc with our group the Warring Women of Zion: Brittany, Amber, Maggie, Samantha, Alicia, Tara, Lindsay, and Jade. I will always hold you dear to my heart! It was the first time I saw the words God gave me to come to life in your responses!

JUST BREATHE

# BREATHE IN MORE OF ME

## GOD
## JEHOVAH JIREH
## THE HOLY SPIRIT
## THE MIGHTY POWERFUL GOD

To breathe means to inhale and exhale. It's my purpose to inhale more of our Mighty Powerful God and then in return exhale it out to others. My prayer has been for this study to bring at least one person closer to God. Then it was worth writing it. This is a five-week study to take you on the Israelites journey to the Promised Land and parallel it to your own personal walk with the Lord.

# ABOUT

## BIBLE STUDY FORMAT:

Over five weeks, each day, you will read a lesson, look up and read scriptures, and answer questions through journaling prompts.

## BIBLE STUDY OVERVIEW:

### WEEK 1: REFLECT

Andrea opens with an opportunity for you to be honest and real with God. She guides you to tell God what's keeping you from diving all-in with Him. Andrea helps you see and acknowledge that His presence is everywhere and He's right by your side.

### WEEK 2: RINSE

Andrea brings you back to your salvation and helps you find your identity in Christ. She helps you recognize the "Egypts" that hold you back. Andrea helps you think back on all your experiences with God that will ignite His fire in your heart.

### WEEK 3: RESTORE

You will examine your heart and forgive those who've wronged you, and will learn to forgive yourself for poor decisions and mistakes. Andrea helps you realize your past is part of your purpose, and how God will qualify the called.

## WEEK 4: REAP

Andrea teaches that God wants you ready to fight the spiritual war wearing His armor, which is perfectly designed to keep you strong and safe. Andrea helps you recognize that you cannot allow your relationship with the Lord to become a checklist of do's and don'ts; instead, seek Him and allow Him to change your heart to want to do it for the Lord. You will then identify the fruit of the spirit and how they are living proof for anyone walking with the Lord. Andrea helps you get full understanding of what full dependency on Christ means: following Him by pillar at night and clouds by day, along with trusting Christ and allowing Him to be your daily bread. Andrea helps you see you have then tasted and see that the Lord is good!

## WEEK 5: REVIVE

Andrea teaches the power of prayer and how He wants everyone to pray about all things with His authority. Andrea emphasizes time in the wilderness and its necessity to teach them about God's attributes and His ways. She helps you accept that His plans are bigger and better for you than they could ever imagine. Then you are ready to take that leap of faith and cross over into the Jordan River with Christ. You not only learn how to stay afloat and walk on the water with Jesus, but also how to discern Him and His ways as He revives your soul.

# WEEK 1:

# REFLECT –
# JOURNALING

## SONG RECOMMENDATION
## FOR WORSHIP:

*"Here's my Heart"* by Lauren Daigle

"Voice of God" by Dante Bowe featuring,
Stephany Gretzinger and Chandler Moore

# EVERY DAY –

We will laugh.

We will ponder on a decision.

We might cry.

We'll be annoyed and might even get angry.

We will be impatient.

We may even feel a rush of excitement
from time to time.

We'll feel hurried.

We'll get hungry.

We'll wish we were skinnier, and then
we'll feel bad about ourselves as we stuff our
faces with Reese's Peanut Butter Cups.

We'll be jealous.

We'll possibly tell a lie or exaggerate.

We'll get tired.

We'll feel overwhelmed.

# WEEK 1: DAY 1
## WHERE AM I WITH GOD?

# YOUR ALARM BEEPS...

...you barely open your eyes and reach for your phone to press snooze. You roll over and quickly drift back to sleep. The annoying sound begins again, and you hit snooze once more. Eventually, you choose to get up and begin your day. You know in the back of your mind, there's an ongoing list of tasks that must get done throughout the day. From the moment your feet hit the floor, you're striving for completion of all the daily mundane things that have filled up your schedule and day.

For all of us, the days cram into one another and then before we realize it, it's been months and summer is almost here.

In a 24-hour day, minus the six hours we get to sleep (eight - if we're lucky), we have 18 hours to live this thing called – LIFE. 18 hours a day to do all the things we need or think we need to get done. But do we stop and wonder where God is in this? Do we even think about HIM in our 18 productive hours?

I challenge you today to stop and ask yourself, "How far am I from God?" He's always there right by our side. We create the distance from Him. We forget what He's done for us on the cross and in our pasts and look the other way.

We feel that strong God-tug and occasionally include Him in our busyness. Sometimes that tug is so strong, we dive all-in and do everything we can think of to grow closer to God. Throughout our Christian walk with Christ, we will have many seasons and terrain. We'll stand on the mountaintops and other times we'll be in the valleys.

At times, our situations will be so unfair and painful that we don't want to give Him a second of our day because we can't bear to go into our hearts or in our minds. Maybe we know our decisions have distanced us from God and we are too ashamed to crawl back on our hands and knees for forgiveness. And then sometimes, we think we are trying our hardest to grow in HIM, yet we feel nothing. This is when we doubt everything we've ever believed.

So, where are you today?

Today is a good day to write a letter to God. Tell Him what makes you afraid, why you're angry with Him, what you feel hopeless about, and what you've prayed for that still brings tears to your eyes. Tell Him what brings you heartache and tell Him the truth of what you think about Him and His Word (be honest).

Tell Him if you're grateful and/or humbled that for the first time in a long time you know you are doing what He wants. Tell Him how thankful you are of all the blessings He's given you. Tell Him how amazing He is. Tell Him how much you love Him and how much you need Him.

Or tell Him how hard this is for you because maybe you've been avoiding Him like the plague.

HE ALREADY KNOWS WHERE YOU ARE,
HE JUST WANTS TO SEE IF YOU ARE READY TO TALK.

# WEEK 1: DAY 1
# APPLICATION

Read these scriptures and then write your letter to God.

## PSALM 139: 2 (NIV)

*You know when I sit down and when I rise-up;
you discern my thoughts from afar.*

## PSALM 139:13-16 (ESV)

*For you formed my inward parts; you knitted me
together in my mother's womb.*

*I praise you, for I am fearfully and wonderfully made.
Wonderful are your works; my soul knows it very well.
My frame was not hidden from you, when I was being
made in secret, intricately woven in the depths of the earth.
Your eyes saw my unformed substance;
in your book were written, every one of them,
the days that were formed for me, when as
yet there was none of them.*

DAY 1

Dear God,

_____

_____

_____

_____

_____

_____

_____

_____

_____

_____

## WEEK 1: DAY 2
## AM I GROWING CLOSER TO GOD?

# WHICH BEST DESCRIBES YOU RIGHT NOW?

## YES

I've been doing these things to grow closer to God.

## NO

There's more I could be doing to grow closer to God.

## I DON'T KNOW

I think I am going through the motions, but my heart isn't in it.

It's OKAY to be honest and admit when we are growing closer or falling further away from God. However, you answered the title of today's study, this will set the stage for the next few weeks as you study His Word and seek Him for wisdom, healing, direction, or even joy.

## THE BIGGEST QUESTIONS I ASKED MYSELF OVER THE YEARS ARE:

How do I get faith like hers?
How do I see or hear God like they do?
How do I get out of this rut that I'm in?
What am I doing wrong because I don't hear Him like they do?
How do I get on God's path for me?
How do I hear Him speak to me?
How do I know what God's will is for my life?
How do I know I'm where He wants me?
And How do I get from right here to over there?

There's been days when I was jealous of watching others rejoice with our Lord because I hadn't experienced Him in the ways they had described. I thought I must have done something bad or took a wrong turn somewhere for me to be where I was because nothing was fair or seemed right. It felt as though the world was against me. I couldn't understand or fathom why my life events were leading me down a road of heartaches, pain, and destruction when it appeared everyone else's paths were full of bliss and fairy dust. During those seasons of my life, I can honestly say there were times I was seeking the Lord and there were times I was just going through the motions.

Those big questions I've asked myself seem to be what most of us think when we compare ourselves to others. I feel sometimes our churches try to teach us "HOW to Grow Closer to GOD," but until we believe in faith, dive into His Word, learn of His attributes and His ways, and pray without ceasing - we won't "get" it.

Being a Christian is HARD. It's so much more than I thought. Our relationship with God can be tangible every single day if we want it to be. We are fighting against our flesh and the lies of the enemy. And the last thing the enemy wants is for us to cross over into uninhibited faith with our Lord and Savior.

# WEEK 1: DAY 2
# APPLICATION

Look up these scriptures and answer the prompts.

## MATTHEW 7:7-9

## JAMES 4:8A

## PSALM 145:8

I want you to use today's journaling time to think about what your actions are or should be for you to grow closer to God. No answer is a wrong answer.

Ask our Heavenly Father HOW He wants you to grow closer to Him. He is our ultimate teacher, and He will guide you along this personal journey over the next few weeks.

Seek His Face. The Bible says in Matthew 7:7

## ASK, SEEK, KNOCK, AND THE DOOR WILL OPEN TO YOU.

So, begin this study with asking Him to help you GROW CLOSER to Him.

What are some things / areas in my life I need to work on?

_____

_____

_____

_____

Should I ask forgiveness for sins, behaviors, etc.?

_____

_____

_____

_____

Should I ask God to help me have self-control, so I don't do them anymore?

_____

_____

_____

_____

Do I have a daily quiet time set aside to be alone with God?

_____

_____

_____

_____

## SOMETIMES WE WANT TO DO ALL THESE THINGS, PUTTING THEM INTO ACTION IS WHERE IT GETS HARD.

# WEEK 1: DAY 3
## WHAT CAUSES ME TO DOUBT HIM?

1. When do I fall and take two steps back in my walk with Christ?

2. What is happening around me that makes me question everything I've ever believed?

3. What makes me lose faith or hope all together?

The enemy is smart. He tells us the most elaborate lies to convince us to take steps in the direction directly opposite of God. Satan is real. He hates all who follow Jesus and will do anything in his power to keep us from turning our lives over to Jesus and to keep us from growing closer to Him while we are here on earth.

ENEMY.
Noun, a person who is actively opposed or hostile to someone or something.

Satan will place doubt and fear in us because those are the most powerful ways to pull us away from God. I doubt when the problem seems like a mountain, when a situation seems impossible, when the world tells me "no", when I'm tired and weary, when all I see is hurt, pain, and darkness, and when I allow my problem to become bigger than my God.

I fall back into my self-pity-party that those good things will never happen for me, that I'm not good enough, that He doesn't love me like that, or He does BIG things for those people but not for me. I begin to think things like I'll never have a "K-Love" praise like those on the radio, or it just isn't in the cards for me to have a happy ending. The list goes on and on.

When my first marriage fell apart, I lost my identity and had to grieve the dreams I had for myself and for my future. I questioned where God was in my life.

When my sister-in-law, Kerri, passed away from a rare liver cancer, I wasn't sure where My God was then because she was the most inspiring person I'd ever known. I couldn't fathom or understand why she needed to die so young. When I watched my in-laws go through the HARDEST stages of grief two years after losing their daughter, I questioned, "Where ARE YOU GOD?!" I witnessed the pain that took over their lives and tore them up from the inside out.

And when my husband, Brian, and I tried for over three and half years to have a baby, there were many of days and nights I questioned where this Powerful God was!

Satan wants us to think God has forgotten about us and that we are all alone. He wants us to FEAR.

So, when do I fall and take 2 steps back? It's when life hurts. It's when I have no control and have to give God the control. It's when He's silent and He's making me wait. It's when I see pure chaos and the world says no - that's impossible.

Doubt will cripple us. Doubt distorts our view or hides God's plan for us while it keeps us held in bondage. Doubt isolates us and even paralyzes us. We must know how to recognize it, how to expect it, and how to rebuke it.

# WEEK 1: DAY 3
# APPLICATION

Look up these scriptures and answer the prompts.

 JAMES 1:6

MATTHEW 17:20

I encourage you to look at your life from when you were little until today. Take time to journal out these thoughts.

Take some time to ask our loving Father to forgive you of the doubt you have held onto to for so long.

Through the difficulties of life, what specifically has caused you to doubt God?

_____

_____

_____

_____

What are those key moments or events that have caused you to question where our mighty and powerful God was in your life?

_____

_____

_____

_____

What are you doubting God for today?

_____

_____

_____

_____

_____

HE CANNOT SHOW US HOW BIG HE
IS IF WE DOUBT HIS GREATNESS!

# WEEK 1: DAY 4
## HAVE I FELT HIS PRESENCE?

## YOU ARE DRIVING...

...as you look out into the blue sky, you see a rainbow. It takes your breath away by how beautiful it is and the magnitude of it.

### THAT'S GOD.

You're reading your Bible and a scripture captivates your heart and resonates in your soul. It brings so much peace over you, and instantly you feel a true joy from within.

### THAT'S GOD.

You sit in church and it appears the preacher is speaking directly at you. His words are piercing your heart while tears are flowing down your cheeks.

### THAT'S GOD.

You hear a praise and worship song in the car on your way to work. The lyrics reflect your thoughts and life like a mirror.

### THAT'S GOD.

You get the right phone call at the right moment to brighten up your day or to give you encouragement.

### THAT'S GOD.

You receive a job offer without having to search for it. It literally falls into your lap.

### THAT'S GOD.

You are loved by strangers and cared for without questions. They don't know you, yet they portray God's love towards you.

### THAT'S GOD.

You hear that soft voice in your head that says, "Trust me."

## THAT'S GOD.

You hear that same soft voice again, but this time it says, "Be Still."

## THAT'S GOD.

You dream of godly or heavenly things, and your spirit doesn't rest until you seek the meaning while you pray for God to show you what that dream meant.

## THAT'S GOD.

You are being prayed over aloud and tears flow from your heart and out from your eyes as your body gets tingly.

## THAT'S GOD.

You look at a newborn baby; their details are so intricate and precise. You are in awe of His creation.

## THAT'S GOD.

And then you sing one of your favorite praise and worship songs with your arms held high, your eyes are closed, and your soul rejoices before the Lord.

## THAT'S GOD.

He goes before us and lays out our steps. He's right there at every intersection of thoughts and decisions. And He's waiting on us to acknowledge His presence and to dive in deeper.

## HIS PRESENCE IS ALL AROUND US.

# WEEK 1: DAY 4
# APPLICATION

Read these scriptures and complete the prompts.

## PSALM 16: 9 (NIV)

*In their heart's humans plan their course, but the Lord establishes their steps.*

## PSALM 139:7-12 (NIV)

*Where can I go from your Spirit?*
*Where can I flee from your presence?*
*If I go up to the heavens, you are there;*
*if I make my bed in the depths, you are there*
*If I rise on the wings of the dawn, if I settle on the far side o*
*the sea, even there your hand will guide me, your right hand*
*will hold me fast.*
*If I say, "Surely the darkness will hide me and the light*
*become night around me," even the darkness will not be*
*dark to you; the night will shine like the day, for darkness is*
*as light to you.*

# DAY 4

Take some time to journal as many encounters of God, His Son, and His Holy Spirit you can recall. You may have only a few, yet you may have too many to count. Recalling the times, you've felt his presence is important in our walks with Him. If you are like me, you may be surprised how often we take for granted the times He's shown us His presence! The Bible says He is always with us, but sometimes He manifested Himself in tangible ways.

_____

_____

_____

_____

_____

_____

_____

_____

_____

_____

_____

# WEEK 1: DAY 5
## DO I BELIEVE HE IS WHO HE SAYS HE IS?

 JOHN 3:16 (NIV)

*For God so loved the world He gave us his begotten son to die a gruesome death to save us and bring life everlasting life into us.*

What does this verse mean exactly? God created us in His image because He found favor in us. He created us, then sets us free into this world to grow up and experience all His creations. He does this with expectations that we will look up to Him for guidance and direction and reciprocate the real unconditional love that seeps out from Him. He gives us the choice. I guess what satisfaction would He have if we were programmed to automatically praise Him?

Why did He have to die a gruesome death to save us? He had to die because there is sin and wicked in this world. We then get side-tracked and pulled into different directions and don't look to Him for help. Sometimes it happens so subtle, we don't realize it. Sometimes the directions we take are so far away from Him, it seems impossible to get back.

How does God bring us everlasting life? He brings it by His grace. He calls for us individually to a personal relationship with Him! There's nothing we can do to earn it. Nothing we can do to get it. It's free monetarily, but to receive it we must die to self. We

# DAY 5

acknowledge that we are sinners and we need His grace to make it through this journey called life! We fully surrender our control over our lives and make Him our savior! He becomes our King. Our Father. Our Lord. Our Redeemer. Our Provider. Our Comforter. Our Healer. The list goes on and on, 70+ titles in the Bible to be exact.

So, do you believe it? Do you deep down like soul searching believe it? Do you believe that He's chosen you?

## YES! YOU!

He wants you to yearn after him. He wants to share with you plans He has for you. He wants to reveal Himself to you. He's a gentleman and will wait as long as it takes until you realize what offer has been on the table that you've yet to take seriously or take to the next level.

# WEEK 1: DAY 5
# APPLICATION

Look up these scripture, journal your thoughts
on who He is to you and if you believe it all.

PSALM 8:1

PSALM 16:2

PSALM 18:1-3

PSALM 23:1-6

PSALM 104:1

ROMANS 1:16-17, 20

COLOSSIANS 1:15-23

2 THESSALONIANS 3:3-5

Do I believe GOD really is who the Bible says He is?

_____

_____

_____

_____

_____

Do I believe He really exists and died for me?

_____

_____

_____

_____

_____

And to my friend who is doubting and questioning His existence, I pray that He will reveal Himself to you during this study in a supernatural way. That you would know without a doubt who He is and where you stand with Him! I pray that your heart will burst with freedom as you trust Him and walk hand in hand with Him!

## I PROMISE YOU, IF YOU GO THROUGH THIS STUDY WITH AN OPEN MIND AND AN OPEN HEART, HE WILL SHOW UP AND CAPTURE YOUR HEART.

# WEEK 2:

# RINSE –
# COMING OUT OF EGYPT

## SONG RECOMMENDATION FOR WORSHIP:

*"You Say" by Lauren Daigle*

*"How He Loves" by David Crowder Band*

*"Reckless Love" by Cory Asbury*

*"Thank you" by Jesus Fellowship Songs*

# WEEK 2: DAY 6

We were all born with the sinful nature. If we don't recognize this truth and surrender to Jesus as our Lord and Savior, then we will live our lives on earth feeding the sinful desires of man. We'll be trapped into the bondage of sin where we'll never be free. Our soul will be held captive; therefore, we'll be a slave to fear, lust, drugs, money, vanity, and even power.

The Bible says the Israelites were being held captive in Egypt for over 400+ years, yet God still heard their cries for help. God sent Moses to deliver them out of their bondage. Our lives before Christ as our Savior and the sins we struggle with are "our Egypt." God sent His Holy Spirit to draw us near and allow Jesus to save and deliver us from our bondage.

## JESUS DIED FOR US TO LIVE.

Under the old testament laws, God had instructed the Israelites on how to perform sacrifices to be cleansed of their sins. In the books of Deuteronomy, Leviticus, and Numbers, we learn about the offerings and what animals were used to shed their blood to cover the sins of God's people. All the animals were to be clean, unblemished animals.

I often think of how the sacrifices were gory; and for the longest time, I couldn't understand why God designed this way. If you've ever gone hunting for deer or elk, then you can visualize the process to offer animals as a sacrifice. I've only gone duck hunting once, years ago. The sight and smell of blood makes me nauseous. I have no desire to go deer hunting.

It must have been daunting to live under the old testament laws, performing sacrifice after sacrifice to atone for sins. Seriously, think about how often we sin in a week's time? I'd be at the altar every day just slaying animals! Thank goodness I was born during the Church Age.

God had a new plan when He sent us His son, Jesus, into the world. Jesus is the Lamb of God who takes away the sins of the world. He's our perfect unblemished lamb that sheds His blood as the ultimate sacrifice for those who believe and follow Him. Our sins were nailed on the cross with Him. Our bondage, addictions, love of money, self-righteousness, words, jealousy, and our pride were nailed on the cross that day the Savior of the world was crucified.

All our "Egypts"—are forever cleansed because of Jesus! Every single sin we'll commit was defeated on the cross before we were even born! Believers can say now that they are dead to sin and alive in Christ! When we choose Christ, the sin cannot hold us captive any longer. We will struggle occasionally in sin, especially if we continue to feed and entertain it; but Jesus gave us the power to stop because of what Jesus did on the cross!

Jesus, the ultimate last sacrifice, puts an end to our strongholds, bad habits and desires, or addictions. God knew we needed a Savior, and He knew one final sacrifice would put an end to the death and destruction of sin.

## HE'S RESCUED US OUT OF EGYPT.

We're all on different paths and journeys with God. Some of us didn't come to know Christ as our Savior until we were much later in age. It's very common for us to make that commitment with God, but years pass before we truly understand what it means to walk with the Lord in a relationship with Him. Our journeys with Christ all look different, but one thing remains the same—we all reached a point when we decided we needed Christ!

We'll eventually reach a point with God where He'll nudge us to begin the sanctification process, AKA the "dying-to-self" process. He wants us to learn how to be more like Him and how to be alive in Christ Jesus. Our struggles don't magically disappear instantly once we become Christians. It takes full commitment and lots of prayer while we seek Him with our whole hearts for Him to begin a new work in us. Our struggles will slowly lose power over us. The "dying-to-self" process is not an easy task, nor does it happen overnight. It's a continual process that God created to direct us so He can change us from the inside out. Think of it as MORE of Him and LESS of me. Paul says, to live is Christ, to die is gain. Our lives should be lived for Him, through Him, to Him, with Him. He wants everything we do to include Him and be about Him! When we try to look more like Jesus, our daily assignment of exterminating our sins may look like the classic game of whack-a-mole.

For too long I was lukewarm Christian in so many areas. I wanted to grow with God but didn't know how. That's why I wrote this study - I want people to know how to grow into a mature son and daughter of OUR KING and not stay trapped in their own sins or pasts.

# WEEK 2: DAY 6
# APPLICATION

Take some time and look up these scriptures, and journal what the Lord shows you through His word as you answer the questions.

## EXODUS 2:23-24

## EXODUS 3:1-17

## MATTHEW 27: 32-54

## ROMANS 5:12-19

## ROMANS 6:1-14

What are some of your "Egypts" that were nailed up on the cross with Jesus?

_____

_____

_____

_____

_____

_____

_____

How do you feel when you stop and think about what Christ did for you?

_____

_____

_____

_____

_____

_____

Can you recall a time when you surrendered to God's calling and came out of Egypt? If yes, please describe it. If no, what is keeping you from that decision?

_____

_____

_____

_____

_____

# WEEK 2: DAY 7
# THE RED SEA

When the Israelites were on their way out of Egypt, God guided their every move with Moses as their leader. Pharaoh changed his mind at the last minute and ordered his army and chariots to stop them. The Israelites came upon a large body of water known as the Red Sea with the Egyptian Army at their heels. Moses raised his staff with full trust and belief in God's faithfulness, and at that profound moment the Red Sea parted. The Israelites could escape and be freed. The Red Sea was a direct pathway to get them from where they were once held captive to where God was ultimately bringing them to the Promised Land. There was only one way out, and they watched before their very eyes as God of the universe performed one of the greatest miracles on earth.

## THERE WAS NO GOING BACK. THERE WAS NO MISTAKE.
## IT WAS DONE. IT WAS FINISHED.
## NO MORE BONDAGE IN EGYPT.

Our salvation happens when we surrender to Christ, and become alive in Him. Once we ask Christ Jesus to be our Savior and believe in our hearts, He cleanses us and makes us new. He is the only way we can leave Egypt.

Then, our baptism is an outward representation of dying to sin as we become washed clean. Christ makes us new again. He takes us out of our bondage -out of our Egypt - and gives us a new life. But there's more.

God has a Divine path, a will for us on Earth. He wants us in the Promise Land with Him!

Just like Pharaoh tried everything he could to stop the Israelites from escaping, Satan will try everything to keep us from turning to Christ. Especially when he knows how powerful our testimony will be to turn more people towards Christ. When we buy into the lies that we aren't good enough, we're too far invested into the sin, God will never forgive me, or I've messed up too bad; we are turning back towards Egypt. We aren't trusting God will hold the waters back for us to cross. We tell ourselves that in Egypt, we'll be fed and have a place to sleep. We forget about the oppression and lostness. We push back the desire to know if God really exists because we're scared. We fear the unknown. And in Egypt, we know we've survived this long, so we'll probably be able to survive a little longer. We aren't believing in God's Power or His greatness. This is where faith comes in. We won't know until we try to take that first leap. As we take each step, we'll see Him hold the waters back!

# WEEK 2: DAY 7
# APPLICATION

Take some time and look up these scriptures, journal what the Lord shows you through His word as you answer the questions.

EXODUS 14:1-31

MATTHEW 3:11-17

2 CORINTHIANS 5:17

ROMANS 10:9-10

JOHN 3:16-17

What does it mean to you to be made new in Christ?

_____

_____

_____

_____

_____

_____

Sometimes we get jaded, and the significance of what Jesus did for us slips our minds. If you're like me, that happens all too often. Sometimes I forget what took place the moment He died for me. Reflect on that for a moment and write your thoughts or a prayer.

_____

_____

_____

_____

_____

Put into your own words what the statement, "It is finished." means to you regarding your salvation with the Lord.

_____

_____

_____

_____

_____

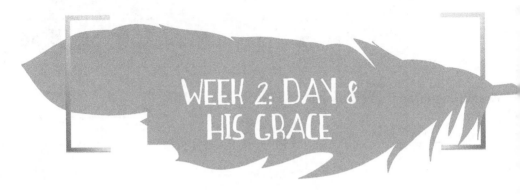

# WEEK 2: DAY 8
# HIS GRACE

GRACE is the free and unmerited favor of God, as manifested in the salvation of sinners and the bestowal of blessings.

I can't even fathom or describe into words HOW GREAT THOU ART! His grace surpasses all understanding. I will never understand how much God loves me. I picture Him cradling my face with His hands as He looks me in the eye and says, "My child, I love you THIS much. Put your focus on me! There's nothing you can do that I haven't already forgiven. I died for you, my child, so you can have life! I knew you couldn't do life alone! So, here I am!"

God wants us to stay attached to Jesus in this life on earth. It's our duty or our calling and He's provided us a way by grace! I heard this analogy and since then, it's helped me grasp His love and grace in exponential ways.

GOD = OWNER OF THE VINEYARD.
JESUS = THE VINE.
US = THE BRANCHES.
FRUIT = THE RESULT OF BEING CONNECTED
TO THE VINE AND FULL OF TRUE JOY.

# DAY 8

The entire goal or cycle that God created for us to dwell in unity with Him all is centered on grace. He created us. He sent a savior for us. God gives us freedom in Him and eternity with Him through grace. We need not do anything to earn it. We only have to accept it and stay attached. As we stay attached and grow with Him we'll begin to produce fruit. After a harvest of some fruit, pruning prepares the branches for more fruit in due time. As long as we stay attached, He does it all. He's the owner of the vineyard. He makes sure we get the proper sunlight, water, and tends to the areas in our life that need pruning. He does this all because of GRACE!

## WE CANNOT HAVE VICTORY IN OUR STRUGGLES UNLESS WE ALLOW HIS GRACE TO PRUNE US AND MAKE US MORE LIKE HIM.

When God worked in my heart and guided me to show grace to someone who had hurt me deep in my soul years ago, it was at that moment I looked back to Him and realized what He did for me. Our sinful nature should keep us so far from our creator, yet He loves and wants a relationship with us anyway. We don't deserve it. We don't deserve any part of this life nor any of the privileges we obtain. God loves us that much!! Grace is the essence of our FATHER!

# WEEK 2: DAY 8
# APPLICATION

Take some time and reflect on these
scriptures, journal what the Lord shows you.

 2 CORINTHIANS 12:8-9

ROMANS 3:22-25A

EPHESIANS 2:8-9

EPHESIANS 4:6-7

Try to describe His Love and what it means to you.

_____

_____

_____

_____

What does grace mean to you?

_____

_____

_____

How have you been able to show His grace to someone in your life? We are called to be the hands and feet of Jesus. Maybe someone needs to see grace from you so Jesus can shine brightly in a tangible way.

_____

_____

_____

_____

How can you show grace to someone this week?

_____

_____

_____

_____

_____

# WEEK 2: DAY 9
# THE VEIL WAS TORN

## -SEND A HELPER

## HEBREWS 6:19 (NIV)

*"We have this hope as an anchor for the soul, firm and secure. It enters the inner sanctuary behind the curtain."*

The moment Christ died on the cross; the veil was torn in the temple that separated the people from the Holy of Holies. In old testament law, people were unclean and not worthy to be in God's presence. Only the high priest could go behind the curtain to present offerings. That curtain or veil was torn in half the moment Christ died. Scripture says ground shook, and the veil was torn. We have direct access to our Father now.

When Jesus appeared to the apostles after His resurrection, He explained to them He was sending us a Helper. The Helper would live inside us, interpret to us His discernment, and give us hope. We have Jesus in us, and we can talk to Him throughout the day. The hope that God gives us is an anchor for our soul because it comes from behind the curtain. It comes from our Father himself.

# DAY 9

Sometimes, I feel like I'm drowning in life's storms. The water swells up and sometimes crashes over my head. I must remind myself that I'm alive in Christ and He's my anchor keeping me afloat. I must remember that I'm not alone in this world, and I can find my energy and drive to become an overcomer through Christ. He's my cornerstone.

## CHRIST BREATHES LIFE INTO ME.

Even when I don't know what prayers to pray, the Bible says His Spirit in me intercedes for me through wordless groans. That same power is in us that rose Christ from the dead. So, when faced with difficult situations or decisions, we must remember who we have in us to help guide us to make the right choices.

# WEEK 2: DAY 9
# APPLICATION

Take some time and reflect on these scriptures:
Read and answer these questions in journal form.

COLOSSIANS 2:5

JOHN 14: 15-17

JOHN 14: 26

JOHN 10: 1-18

What does it mean to you that Jesus sent us a Helper?

_____

_____

_____

_____

_____

Do you call upon our Helper for guidance and help in this world?

_____

_____

_____

_____

Have you sat long enough in silence to allow His soft sweet tender voice to have dominion over any other thought?

_____

_____

_____

_____

Slowly, over time you will recognize His voice! I challenge you to talk to Him daily. Be still before the Lord and hear His voice. It will be life changing!

_____

_____

_____

_____

# WEEK 2: DAY 10
## SPIRITUAL FULLNESS IN CHRIST

First read this portion of Colossians in The Passion Translation.
I like the way it's worded.

## COLOSSIANS 2:6-15 (TPT)

*"In the same way you received Jesus our Lord and Messiah by faith, continue your journey of faith, progressing further into your union with him! Your spiritual roots go deeply into his life as you are continually infused with strength, encouraged in every way. For you are established in the faith you have absorbed and enriched by your devotion to him! Beware that no one distracts you or intimidates you in their attempt to lead you away from Christ's fullness by pretending to be full of wisdom when they're filled with endless arguments of human logic. For they operate with humanistic and clouded judgments based on the mindset of this world system, and not the anointed truths of the Anointed One. For he is the complete fullness of deity living in human form.*

*And our own completeness is now found in him. We are completely filled with God as Christ's fullness overflows within us. He is the Head of every kingdom and authority in the universe! Through our union with him we have experienced circumcision of heart. All of the guilt and power of sin has been cut away and is now extinct because of what Christ, the Anointed One, has accomplished for us. For we've been buried with him into his death. Our "baptism into death" also means we were raised with him when we believed in God's resurrection power, the power that raised him from death's realm.*

*This "realm of death" describes our former state, for we were held in sin's grasp. But now, we've been resurrected out of that "realm of death" never to return, for we are forever alive and forgiven of all our sins! He canceled out every legal violation we had*

*on our record and the old arrest warrant that stood to indict us. He erased it all—our sins, our stained soul—he deleted it all and they cannot be retrieved! Everything we once were in Adam has been placed onto his cross and nailed permanently there as a public display of cancellation. Then Jesus made a public spectacle of all the powers and principalities of darkness, stripping away from them every weapon and all their spiritual authority and power to accuse us. And by the power of the cross, Jesus led them around as prisoners in a procession of triumph. He was not their prisoner; they were his!"*

## WE HAVE THE FREEDOM TO WORSHIP JESUS WITH OUR MIND, BODY, AND SPIRIT.

We have the freedom to ask Him to rule over our lives, and we have the space to look forward instead of being stuck in our pasts. Christ died to free us of our sins. So, we could have a relationship with Him. To know Him personally and intimately as our heavenly Father. We aren't bound to the shackles of sins, strongholds, addictions, medications, lies, doubt, and shame.

## AS A BELIEVER, WE ARE FREE FROM EGYPT.

Jesus gives us grace. He meets us in the trenches and picks us up and carries us home. He puts us under His wing and brings us to the next place. Our Father does this lovingly, not condemning. He works from the inside out, revealing Himself to us all the while changing us and renewing our minds.

Jesus loves to bless us; He will do so as He sees fit in His way. He won't bless us with something or someone if someone or something to become our little "god."

He knows our hearts better than we do. He wants us to depend on HIM and will bless us if we keep Him first. Jesus wants your love even when the answer is no or not right now. When we are obedient, He blesses tenfold in His ways and His timing.

# WEEK 2: DAY 10
# APPLICATION

Re-read Colossians 2:6-15, Answer these questions in journal form.

## COLOSSIANS 2:6-15 (TPT)

"New Life in Christ,"

"In the same way you received Jesus our Lord and Messiah by faith, continue your journey of faith, progressing further into your union with him! Your spiritual roots go deeply into his life as you are continually infused with strength, encouraged in every way. For you are established in the faith you have absorbed and enriched by your devotion to him! Beware that no one distracts you or intimidates you in their attempt to lead you away from Christ's fullness by pretending to be full of wisdom when they're filled with endless arguments of human logic. For they operate with humanistic and clouded judgments based on the mindset of this world system, and not the anointed truths of the Anointed One. For he is the complete fullness of deity living in human form.

And our own completeness is now found in him. We are completely filled with God as Christ's fullness overflows within us. He is the Head of every kingdom and authority in the universe! Through our union with him we have experienced circumcision of heart. All of the guilt and power of sin has been cut away and is now extinct because of what Christ, the Anointed One, has accomplished for us. For we've been buried with him into his death. Our "baptism into death" also means we were raised with him when we believed in God's resurrection power, the power that raised him from death's realm.

This "realm of death" describes our former state, for we were held in sin's grasp. But now, we've been resurrected out of that "realm of death" never to return, for we are forever alive and forgiven of all our sins! He canceled out every legal violation we had on our record and the old arrest warrant that stood to indict us. He erased it all—our sins, our stained soul—he deleted it all and they cannot be retrieved! Everything we once were in Adam has been placed onto his cross and nailed permanently there as a public display of cancellation. Then Jesus made a public spectacle of all the powers and principalities of darkness, stripping away from them every weapon and all their spiritual authority and power to accuse us. And by the power of the cross, Jesus led them around as prisoners in a procession of triumph. He was not their prisoner; they were his!"

What are things you've prayed for, and He didn't answer?

_____

_____

_____

_____

What do you think He was trying (or is trying) to teach you?
"The darkest times in life only last until God's purpose is revealed" is my favorite quote from Dr. Charles Stanley. Think about that quote while answering this question.

_____

_____

_____

_____

What has God blessed you with over the years?
Do you take for granted His goodness?

_____

_____

_____

_____

What does it mean to you to have freedom in Christ?

_____

_____

_____

_____

How would you describe what freedom in Christ is to someone who doesn't believe in Jesus?

_____

_____

_____

_____

# WEEK 3:

# RESTORE - FORGIVENESS & HEALING

## SONG RECOMMENDATION FOR WORSHIP:

*"Egypt" by Corey Asbury & Bethel Music*

*"Goodness of God" by Jen Johnson & Bethel Music*

*"O Come to the Altar" by Elevation Worship*

*"Through all of It" by Colton Dixon*

*"I will follow" by Chris Tomlin*

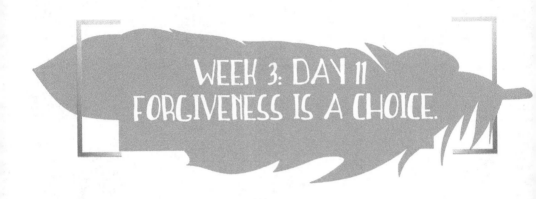

## WEEK 3: DAY 11
## FORGIVENESS IS A CHOICE.

### FORGIVENESS.

A child barges into the room, ranting and raving about how much they hate or heavily dislike their older sibling. The parent asks questions and tries to dig deeper into the situation to figure out what "actually" happened between the two. The parent tells the child to tell their brother or sister they are sorry and love them. The child responds hastily, "But MOM!" or "But DAD!"

*Or maybe I should use this example instead.*

## GOD WANTS YOU TO FORGIVE AND SHOW GRACE TOWARDS SOMEONE WHO HAS HURT YOU TERRIBLY. YOU DON'T WANT TO; YOU REFUSE, BUT GOD WILL CONTINUE TO PRESS YOU UNTIL YOU FINALLY SURRENDER.

After being separated for an entire year from my first husband, he was trying to decide if he wanted me or someone else. I cannot put into words the feelings of rejection that steered my thoughts and actions. God carried me through that awful storm. But God didn't let me off the hook with the excuse, "But he wronged me!" Thankfully, our God

is gracious, and He saw through the pain and hurt in my heart. He knew I wanted to be freed of the pain and rejection. Through multiple attempts of successful prayer sessions and even some Christian counseling sessions, God would not allow me to move forward with Him until forgiveness took place in my heart. The freedom that releases the moment we allow forgiveness to take place is liberating. Only through Christ is this even possible!

We can choose to forgive. We don't deserve God's forgiveness towards us, yet that's the beauty of His unconditional love for us. Whosoever has hurt you mentally, physically, or emotionally probably doesn't deserve your forgiveness either if they haven't turned towards Christ. But it's what we are commanded to do. We must forgive for us to grow closer to Christ. It conditions our hearts for what God has in store for us next. Sometimes it's not fair, and we still want revenge or even an apology. We may even struggle to forgive them, even if they've turned to Christ and begged for forgiveness. Jesus is calling us all to His table to feast, even those who have hurt us. I took a long time to accept that Jesus wants their hearts too! We are to set the example, to be Christlike here on Earth and let go and forgive those who hurt us. To do as He would do, to let go and forgive. If we do not forgive, bitterness, anger, rage, and hostility will hold our hearts captive. We will be the ones suffering because more times than not, they've moved on and forgotten. Our enemy doesn't want us to do anything Christ proclaims. He wants us miserable and lonely. He wants us swirling around in hate and bitterness; he wants to kill, steal, and destroy us. When we forgive, there's an atmospheric shift and angels rejoice with us!

And sometimes, we may need to say it out loud many times in prayer that we've forgiven them. After months and even years later, old feelings can resurface, and we must pray forgiveness over them or the situation again. God wants to help us pull the root of whatever we're holding onto with bitterness or anger about that hurtful topic or person that will hinder us from a pure heart. The jealousy, pride, bitterness, or even hate will destroy our hearts and keep a wedge between Christ and us. Pray for God to identify the roots still planted deep within and begin weeding them out.

# WEEK 3: DAY 11
# APPLICATION

Look up these scriptures about forgiveness,
journal what the Lord reveals to your heart.

## MATTHEW 5: 23-24; 38-45

## MATTHEW 7:12

## MATTHEW 22:39

## ROMANS 12:17-21

## EPHESIANS 4:1-3

DAY 11

Think of an example of when you or someone close to you showed graced and forgave someone? It's the Jesus in you that pushes you to forgive!

_____

_____

_____

_____

_____

_____

_____

_____

_____

_____

_____

_____

# WEEK 3: DAY 12
# MY PAST

Have you ever found yourself wrapped up in self-pity? Have you thrown yourself an actual pity-party? I know my hormones must play a huge role in this, but sometimes it's so easy to get wrapped up in my "woe's me" attitude. Nothing seems to go right. You're tired and fed up. You can't see the light. And your past is haunting you in the mirror. The lies of self-worthlessness are taking over and throwing the worst party on the planet in your very own head! It's so sad, but I've been there so often. And every time I tell myself, "Andrea... snap out of this. Tighten up. Get yourself together. Andrea. Pray. His thoughts are higher than mine!"

## JESUS HAS US ALL ON A DIFFERENT JOURNEY.

I cannot compare my life to anyone else's! Or at least that's what God wants me to do, and I struggle with this simple concept. I may have taken a few detours out of immaturity, selfishness, self-defiant determination, or out of pure stupidity. But regardless, we are on personal journeys. Jesus allows us to decide all-knowing what our choices will cause and how He will intervene and get us back on His path if we're willing to surrender and ask Him for help.

I am 38 years old. Married at 21 and quickly divorced by the age of 24. Single again in my mid-twenties led to a desire to travel while exploring and doing mission work with various organizations. I had finally trusted God had better for me, which led me to get my master's degree and switch professions at 26. Talk about a depressing topic of discussion at my 10-year high school reunion. Nothing was as I thought it would be. Thank you, Jesus, for having better plans for me and giving me a new life! I switched

DAY 12

faiths and was baptized at 25, proclaiming what Jesus did in me at 16; then met my husband today at 26, and we married two years later. We traveled, loved starting our married life together, even while we endured one of the hardest trials in our family as we stood by his sister's side when cancer took her life. Our family went through grieving pains  the dictionary can't even describe. It was eye-opening to watch what my in-laws went through and led me to a deeper understanding of mental health and what depression can do to a family. Then, after much prayer and years of anticipation and waiting on God's timing, we finally had our first child in 2017.

## BUT GOD.

God knew this would be my story and my past. My life's journey would make me who I am today. I now love and embrace my journey because I have grown exponentially. I had to forgive myself for the mistakes I had made, for decisions I made without seeking God, and for doubting how powerful my God is.

We will not grow closer to Him if we can't forgive ourselves. He paid the price and settled it on the cross. It's over. Done. And now He wants to hold us and breathe life back into us.

As an educator, I've taught many students dealt with the worst hands in life. I know now that I do not understand what it is like to be abused and abandoned. Some of you might look at my life and think, *Your past can't hold a candle to mine.*

And you're right, but no matter what your past is, Jesus OVERCAME it! He's sought you through it, and He's here's now wanting to wash you clean. He wants to breathe life into you!

# WEEK 3: DAY 12
# APPLICATION

Look up these scriptures about forgiveness,
reflect on what God wants to teach you.

## DEUTERONOMY 10:20-21

## PROVERBS 3:5-6

## ROMANS 8:28

## PHILIPPIANS 4: 11-13

DAY 12

Describe your journey so far.

_____

_____

_____

_____

Is your life anything that you expected?

_____

_____

_____

_____

Are there any things you've done that you can't get over/ move on from?

_____

_____

_____

_____

When or how has God intervened in your life?

_____

_____

_____

_____

Describe what being content in your life on your journey means to you?

_____

_____

_____

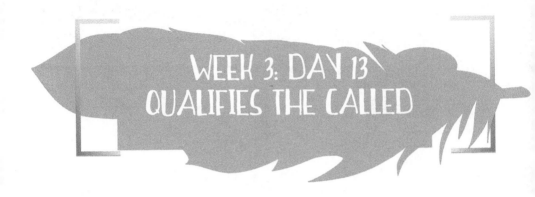

# WEEK 3: DAY 13
# QUALIFIES THE CALLED

God picks the least likely people to become leaders, to change lives, and to move mountains.

## WITH GOD, NOTHING IS IMPOSSIBLE.

You hear that voice in your head saying, "Volunteer." or "Go." or "Serve." or "Write." and you quickly respond with, "I can't." We'll never be ready to do what God has in store for us. We must do it anyway. Trust God and what He has laid befor you is in His divine plan, and He'll guide and help you along the way.

We all have our struggles. What separates me from Christ might differ totally from what you battle with. The beauty is that we all have a past, and we need not be perfect for God to use us. I found this example online.

"Jacob was a cheater, Peter had a temper, David had an affair, Noah got drunk, Jonah ran from God, Paul was a murderer, Gideon was insecure, Miriam was a gossip, Martha was a worrier, Thomas was a doubter, Sara was impatient, Elijah was moody, Moses stuttered, Abraham was old, and Lazarus was dead. God doesn't call the qualified; He qualifies the CALLED!" quoted from livingforjesus.com

I am not a natural writer. But God has called me to write about His love story with us. He's called me to be a disciple and a disciple-maker by encouraging others to grow deeper in their relationship with Him. He gave me the outline of this study one morning in prayer, and then He gave me the words to fill each day's lesson.

When we rely on God to get us through and qualify us for what He has planned, we depend on Him. And that's right where He wants us.

I have struggled with what being a disciple looks like and especially what making disciples look like. I love overseas missions, and Brian and I want to take our son, Payne when he is older. So, I've always thought there's nothing I can do for His kingdom-right now.

I've always heard God say, "Write" for years before I wrote this study. But I never had the confidence to follow through with it. I pushed it back and kept listening to the enemy's lies that I won't be good enough, I'm not an English major, I can't spell worth a darn, and no one will enjoy it. When God called me to write this study, I was scared. Was it silly for me to think I could do it? But seeing God's provision come into fruition is AMAZING!

He's given me confidence and taking that first step to do what He wants me to do is liberating. I can't describe it.

I hope you will pray for God to show you what He wants you to do for His kingdom! Maybe He's called you to sidewalk ministries - serving our community, leading a small group or Sunday school class, to start a prayer group at work, or to help the elderly. Maybe you are to sing for Him or write too!

## WE'VE ALL BEEN GIVEN THE HOLY WORD AS A PRIZED POSSESSION... TO SPREAD HIS LOVE TO OTHERS!

# WEEK 3: DAY 13
# APPLICATION

Look up these scriptures, journal what the Lord shows you through His word as you answer the questions.

## PHILIPPIANS 1:6

## ISAIAH 55:8-9

## 1 THESSALONIANS 5:23-24

## PHILIPPIANS 2:13

## MATTHEW 28: 19-20

What has God been calling you to do, yet you keep making excuses or doubting your abilities?

_____

_____

_____

_____

_____

_____

_____

Why do you think we run or come up with a million and one excuses when we are put outside our comfort zones?

_____

_____

_____

_____

_____

_____

# WEEK 3: DAY 14
# MY PURPOSE

Once God removes our blinders and allows us to see and understand grace, it's then that we can see with fresh eyes like His. Our purpose here on Earth is to grow closer to our God and bring others closer along the way. It's a daily walk with Him. We must entirely depend on Christ for everything. God's will for us is to be molded into the image of His son and to be as much like Jesus as we can. We must forgive others and ourselves for mistakes and poor decisions we've made in the past for us to move forward with Christ.

It's my purpose to take my trials and lessons God taught me through life and share with others. Switching faiths, going through a divorce, changing career paths, battling infertility, grieving my sister-in-law's death, helping my husband's family heal and be restored after her death, and even the daily life struggles of motherhood, marriage, and work are all part of my purpose.

My purpose is to be a living testimony sharing my life at work, with friends, across the street with my neighbors, in my home with my husband and my children, and public grocery shopping or pushing my son on the swing at the local park. Our society can make us feel insignificant and that we don't have a purpose here on Earth. God delights in us every time we tell a message of hope to someone in our path, hurting from something we survived or overcame with Him.

## OUR LIVES BECOME OUR STORIES, AND THESE STORIES BECOME OUR TESTIMONIES, AND TESTIMONIES CHANGE LIVES.

No one else can tell your story better than you. It's your story. It's one of your purposes for why you're walking around the earth. What YOU once struggled in will be someone else's new heartache and trial.

# WEEK 3: DAY 14
# APPLICATION

Look up these scriptures, then go back and answer the questions as you journal. While you are thinking about these questions, ask God to show you comfort, direction, purpose, and healing as you read His word.

 1 SAMUEL 16:7

ISAIAH 41:10

2 CORINTHIANS 1:3-7

JAMES 1:12

1 PETER 1: 6-9

EPHESIANS 4:6

What's your purpose?

_____

_____

_____

_____

What has God allowed you to go through so you might comfort someone else?

_____

_____

_____

_____

How is God trying to change you to be more like His son?

_____

_____

_____

_____

What are areas in your life you battle with?

_____

_____

_____

_____

# WEEK 3: DAY 15
## RESTORING AND REFLECTING

When our hearts and actions are aligned with God's love and principles, we will have the fruits of the Spirit oozing out of us. It's clear that we seek our Father and grow closer to Him because He is making us more like Him.

## GALATIANS 5:22-23 (NIV)

"But the fruit of the Spirit is love, joy, peace, forbearance, kindness, goodness, faithfulness, gentleness, and self-control."

I don't know if you are like me, but I struggle with self-control! "I should get up and do my bible study- but man, I'm tired. I shouldn't eat that cheesecake, or at least not the whole thing!  I shouldn't have said that about her, or maybe I should have been nicer to her. I probably should get off social media and do housework. I should go volunteer somewhere or donate to this cause or another. I need to stop watching this episode and go to bed. I need to be slow to anger and slow to speak. I should pray first before overreacting or being irrational. I should try counting to 10 and praying before I snap at my husband again for the hundredth time. Maybe I shouldn't nag and do it myself. Do I need to be the one to call a truce & forgive first? What if it's me and not just him after all? I shouldn't take my frustrations out on whoever is in the line of fire when I'm stressed and maxed out. I should refrain from using my defense mechanism of denial and look in the mirror and accept that I'm hardheaded and selfish sometimes.

When I'm seeking God, and really in His Word, I notice my thought process changes, and my perspective changes. When I'm going through the motions and do my "Christian checklist," I allow the worldly views and standards to cloud my mind and thoughts, and then it carries over into my actions and attitude.

It's an everlasting struggle. A clue that I'm going through the motions is that self-control is a major battle in my mind. I'm not gentle with my words, and I hold grudges. Sometimes, I get so mad when the McDonald's worker doesn't get my order right!

DAY 15

I secretly rolled my eyes through my teen years when reading scripture about being holy. I struggled to do what was right because I wanted to have fun and experience life. I was a good kid but testing the waters a little always seemed fun.

As I've gotten older, I realize now why all these scriptures are in the Bible. Who am I kidding? Even as an adult in different seasons, I still struggle with it. And I know the same power that rose Jesus from the dead is living inside me too! When I think of the magnitude of that statement; and how God wants all of me and not just part of me. It goes deep down to my core and makes me want to change and be better. Then I feel silly for wanting to do these pointless things that didn't bring me closer to Him. It's a struggle to balance, keeping my body healthy physically, mentally, and spiritually. I've always struggled and finally realized God wants us to be a living witness, and we shouldn't make our brother or sister in Christ stumble. It's all a balance, and too often, I excel in one area, and then the others are lacking.

It's like those memes about adulting or motherhood being hard; living out the Christian life is HARD. It's a constant self-check process and identifying where we are with Christ.

The hope that keeps me crawling back to Christ is that He loves me just the way I am. He knows my temptations and my weaknesses. I'm never going to be perfect. I'm a hot mess most of the time. He knows when I'm going through the motions and when I'm not honest with myself. Knowing all that, He still spreads HIS LOVE around me and helps me see Him more clearly.

He restores me and makes me new, day after day. He never tires of wiping off the dust, dirt, or grime to let His light shine even brighter.

# WEEK 3: DAY 15
# APPLICATION

Look up these scriptures about renewing our minds and molding us to be more like Christ. Journal what the Lord shows you.

 1 PETER 1:13-16

ROMANS 12: 1-2

1 CORINTHIANS 3:16

1 CORINTHIANS 15: 9-11

GALATIANS 5: 13-26

Take some time thinking about the fruits of the Spirit,
and do you see these pouring out you?

_____

_____

_____

_____

Which one do you struggle with most?

_____

_____

_____

_____

How can you work on that fruit of the Spirit this weekend and into next week?

_____

_____

_____

# WEEK 4:

# REAP –
# IN THE WILDERNESS

## SONG RECOMMENDATION FOR WORSHIP:

*"First" by Lauren Daigle*

*"Good Good Father" by Chris Tomlin*

*"Reckless Love" by Cory Asbury*

# WEEK 4: DAY 16
# ARMOR OF GOD

Once we cross the Red Sea and learn of our worth, value, and purpose, we hunger for more. Moses brought the Israelites out of Egypt, and they stayed in the wilderness for forty years before they crossed the Jordan River into the Promised Land. The wilderness is where they learned to depend on God. They understood God's character; they learned how hardheaded they were, they learned how Faithful God was, and soon learned how short their memory was of His faithfulness and goodness.

Fast forward to today, we are just like Israelites. We need to learn how to depend on Jesus for EVERYTHING. We need to know of God's character and His attributes. We need to learn and see how faithful our God is and remember our forgetfulness.

The enemy's schemes and lies will tempt us to doubt and fall away, just like they did. Because of our laziness or dependency on fear, we'll be distant to our Father, just like they were in the wilderness.

DAY 16

Paul instructed us in Ephesians 6 to put on the full armor of God. He wants us to be aware and ready for battle in the spiritual realm. The closer we get to God, the more the enemy will try to pull us down and distract us. He gave us these instructions to teach us to stand in truth with God's righteousness while protecting our hearts. We can wear the readiness of peace as we extinguish flames of evil with our faith. And as a child of God, we fight with the sword of truth, which is His Word.

I was not raised to memorize scripture or to compete in Bible drills. But I am a Christian wife, mother, and daughter who tries to ask, seek, and knock. If my hope is God revealing more and more; I need to memorize His word. It's our sword! It's active and living; it's sacred.

The Israelites didn't have the Holy Spirit living in them as they learned about God, nor was the Holy Spirit in them on their journey to get to the Promise Land. But we do! We have double the ammo to fight the enemy!

# WEEK 4: DAY 16
# APPLICATION

Look up these scriptures, journal your thoughts as you go through the questions.

 HEBREWS 4:12

EPHESIANS 6:10-18

1 CHRONICLES 16:11

Even after God delivered the Israelites out of Egypt after 400 years of oppression and parted the Red Sea for them to cross and escape Pharaoh's army, they still doubted Him.

What are blessings or answered prayers that God has given you,
you may have forgotten?

_____

_____

_____

What's causing you to think God doesn't hear your prayers or that
He can't fix your problem if He's done all those things/blessings for you in the past?

_____

_____

_____

Why is knowing His Word so important to you?

_____

_____

_____

What do you think it means to have the Word of God in your heart?

_____

_____

_____

Identify each part of the armor labeling and briefly describing what it means to you:

BELT                              SHIELD
_____             _____

BREASTPLATE                       HELMET
_____             _____

SANDALS                           SWORD
_____             _____

91

# WEEK 4: DAY 17
## BACK TO BASICS

In Exodus 19 and 20, we learn the glory of the Lord appeared to the Israelites at Mount Sinai about three months after their exile out of Egypt. The Glory of the Lord appeared as a thick cloud covering the mountain along with thunder and lightning. And in Exodus 19:20, The Lord called Moses to the top of the mountain and gave us the ten commandments and 600+ laws for them to follow. If you believed in God, your attitude and behavior reflected religion and all the dos and don'ts of how we should live in the Old Testament days. But since Jesus died to save us out of grace, we don't have the regulations and control that religion once had over us. We want to do what God wants out of our love for Christ. If we look at our walk with Christ as a checklist, we've missed the point and purpose of why He died for us. Nothing I do will make Him love me more or any less!

I learned these as a kid, but I think little about them now as an adult. They are easy to keep commandments. But if I look and think about them, I fail. I have taken these for granted and almost desensitized myself to some. The ones like don't kill, steal, or commit adultery are ones I know and have no desire to do. But some others, if I analyze my thoughts and actions, I break many!

When I have allowed my husband or son to become more important than my relationship with God, I'm breaking the first one! I have said a better or less derogatory version of the Lord's name in vain, and that still doesn't make it okay!! I haven't always tried to go to church and keep Sunday Holy. I can't count the number of times I've been disrespectful to my parents; still, it happens even as an adult. Not covet my neighbor's house, well, social media is the worst outlet for this! We look and subconsciously

compare our lives to our friends or followers and then feel yucky and like a loser when nothing about our lives looks glorious or as glamourous as theirs. I love seeing pictures of my friends' kids growing up, staying in contact with long distant friends, and keeping up with extended family. I love our life and have found contentment with everything we have or don't have; yet I can compare myself without realizing it. I'll be honest; I took a break from social media to focus as I wrote and did this study with friends. I enjoyed the extra time with my family, and I didn't catch myself comparing my life. It was a sweet time to pray for friends and loved ones instead of scrolling the endless feed in a trance while in autopilot.

## WE ARE HUMANS FIGHTING AGAINST OUR FLESH.

We are sinners. And no matter how hard we want to be perfect, we never will be! God loves us just as we are; imperfect vessels with hearts that beat because of Him! We should want to follow or try to follow the ten commandments because we know that's what God wants us to do out of love! He doesn't want us to be robots and only go through the motions. We've missed the whole point if we allow ourselves to have the checklist mentality. When we don't measure up, we'll feel defeated because we failed again and again!

Instead, I need to do a self-check with myself and ask where is my heart with the Lord? Am I doing or seeking Him out of guilt or because I love Him, and I know that's what I need? He changes our desires to want to be more like His.

# WEEK 4: DAY 17
# APPLICATION

Think about the ten commandments or any other standard that God has for us as Christians.

## LET'S LOOK AT THE TEN COMMANDMENTS.(NIV)

Exodus 20:2-3, "I am the Lord your God, who brought you out of Egypt, out of the land of slavery. You shall have no other gods before me."

Exodus 20:4-6, "You shall not make for yourself an idol in the form of anything in heaven above or on the earth beneath or in the waters below. You shall not bow down to them and worship them; for I, the Lord your God, am a jealous God, punishing the children for the sins of the fathers to the third and fourth generations of those who hate me; but showing love to a thousand generations of those who love me and keep my commandments."

Exodus 20: 7, "You shall not misuse the name of the Lord your God, for the Lord will it hold anyone guiltless who misuses his name."

Exodus 20:8, "Remember the Sabbath day by keeping it, Holy."

Exodus 20:12, "Honor your father and your mother, so you may live long in the land that the Lord your God is giving you."

Exodus 20:13, "You shall not murder."

Exodus 20:14, "You shall not commit adultery."

Exodus 20:15, "You shall not steal."

Exodus 20:16, "You shall not give false testimony against your neighbor."

Exodus 20:17, "You shall not covet your neighbor's house. You shall not covet your neighbor's wife, or his manservant or maidservant, his ox or donkey, or anything that belongs to your neighbor."

Are you striving to follow the Ten Commandments out of guilt or fear? Or
are you following them because in your heart you want to please Him and
hear, "Well done, my good and faithful servant?"

_____

_____

_____

How would we explain that our God is a jealous God to a non-believer?

_____

_____

_____

_____

_____

_____

_____

# WEEK 4: DAY 18
## PRAYER -
## BE REAL AND BE OPEN.

When I was younger, I thought praying meant repeatedly reciting pre-written prayers. In high school I discovered the freedom to pray to God from my own heart with my own words. I even journaled my prayers. I continued throughout college and off and on throughout my first marriage.

During my divorce I got serious about my prayer life. I found so much comfort in many of David's Psalms. His heart ached (like mine), and he felt like the world was against him. I made a promise to God that from that point forward, I would make time for Him no matter what was going on in my life. It's one of those milestone moments I placed a marker to remember that I was recommitting my life to the Lord. I would let God do things His way this time!

After living on my own again, I'd wake up and fix myself toast and instant French Vanilla Cappuccino. (I was an apprentice coffee drinker!) I'd get cozy on the futon to dive into His word, reflect on it, and then try to apply it to my life. There were days I was so angry; I screamed out at God in my prayers. I was hurting so badly, and I knew if He knew my heart, then why not just let it all out? My poor neighbors heard it all!

I remember the burdens were lifted immediately off of my shoulders as I finally let out my pain verbally and surrendered to His ways. I think it's okay to be real sometimes.

# DAY 18

He already knows our thoughts before we do. Be open to the Holy Spirit to whisper into your heart. We cannot forget the same power living in us is the same power that rose Jesus from the grave. The Holy Spirit is our helper and our counselor. He intervenes on God's behalf for us when we don't know what to pray.

Pray with your eyes wide open. Pray with authority. Pray with certainty and clarity. Pray bold prayers. Pray intentionally. Pray from the depths of your heart. Pray without ceasing. Pray continually. Pray prayers of thanksgiving.

Pray the Lord's promises over your life. Pray the Lord's promises over your loved ones. Pray prayers to break chains and knock down walls. Pray prayers for strongholds to be released and for healing to take place. Pray for restoration. Pray for peace, hope, and love. Pray alone in your house, hidden from everyone and everything.

Pray with your friends and family. Pray with your kids. Pray at work. Pray while you drive. Pray before bed and before your feet hit the ground in the morning. Pray before you read your Bible. Pray before an important meeting or conversation.

Pray for salvation. Pray for sanctification. Pray for His glory and power to be revealed. Pray for a revival.

## PRAY. ABOUT. EVERYTHING.

# WEEK 4: DAY 18
# APPLICATION

Think about the ten commandments or any other standard that God has for us as Christians. Journal what the Lord reveals to you about yourself and your relationship with Him.

 ROMANS 8:26

EPHESIANS 6:18

1 JOHN 5:14

JAMES 5:13

MARK 11:24

MATTHEW 26:41

MATTHEW 6:9-13

Which of the ways I described how to pray resonates in your heart?  Why?

_____

_____

_____

_____

_____

_____

_____

_____

_____

_____

_____

# WEEK 4: DAY 19
## MANNA & QUAIL
## AND PILLAR BY NIGHT & CLOUD BY DAY.

Begin today's study by reading these scriptures first.

## EXODUS 16
### MANNA AND QUAIL

## DEUTERONOMY 8
### DO NOT FORGET THE LORD

## JOHN 6: 30-51
### JESUS THE BREAD OF LIFE

**DAY 19**

Jesus is our daily bread. We can't store up extra alone time with him to carry us over for another day or two; we need to seek His face daily. Jesus always wants us to keep our eyes on HIM. We do this by reading His word and devotions, working on a bible study, reading commentaries and books of people's experiences with God, watching episodes or listening to podcasts of sermons or interviews. Feed your heart, soul, and mind with knowledge of our Great and Mighty King! Spend time alone with Jesus reading His word, journaling, talking out loud to Him, praying quietly, meditating on scripture, or listening to Christian music or hymns. Carve out a portion of your day to just be you and Him!

## JESUS WILL CHANGE YOUR LIFE!

During our wilderness journey, our goal is to learn of His ways and His time here on earth. We need to dig into His commandments and values. We need to read of His miracles and the Power of the Holy Spirit! If we don't educate ourselves on what it means to be a Christian or about the power behind our amazing God, then we will be like babies following others and doing what they tell us to do. Knowing no better, we will doubt our God's abilities to do the impossible. We'll be lukewarm Christians that waiver with society.

He wants our full attention and to depend entirely on Him for our every need. God calls us to grow spiritually and become mature Christians. It's taking me a while to get this. And I still struggle. The Israelites knew where to go by following the clouds by the day and the pillar of light by night. If we are struggling to understand - how to get on the right path or where God wants us, we need to seek Him daily. Then we'll be on the right track. This was a huge light bulb moment for me. When I finally realized that I'd be exactly where He wants me, it took the fear, doubt, and guesswork out. I could rest better at night knowing I was WHERE HE WANTED AND NEEDED ME! Gradually, He'll steer us in different directions by changing our hearts' desires, aligning people and circumstances, and allowing our eyes to see more like Him. God will take us to new places and on new journeys if we seek Him first.

This newfound wisdom carried over into every aspect of my life! My career path, my family relationships, my health, my goals and dreams, my relationships with my husband, my child & future children, and basically every detail that makes me—Me.

# WEEK 4: DAY 19
# APPLICATION

Refer to the scriptures you read at the beginning
of today's reading.

Take some time to journal what the Lord has shown you today.
Refer to the scriptures you read at the beginning of today's reading.

_____

_____

_____

_____

_____

_____

_____

_____

_____

_____

_____

_____

_____

_____

# WEEK 4: DAY 20
## TASTE AND SEE THE LORD IS GOOD

"Draw near to God, and He draws near to you," James 4:8. This scripture and promise are proven repeatedly in the Bible. If you reach out, He will grab your hand and will walk with you. There have been times, though, when I have cried out to God and felt like He was nowhere to be found. I felt alone. Or He didn't answer my prayer the way I thought He would have. He goes before us (makes plans and a future), He goes with us (carrying us along the way), and He goes behind us (to clean up our mess) for the scripture says, He will not forsake us. Don't give up. Do not listen to our enemy's lies that God doesn't care, or that He doesn't love you enough.

If you push forward, hang on to the anchor of hope, and refuse to quit while you keep your eyes on Jesus - you will see HE is GOOD!

PSALM 34:8 SAYS, TASTE AND SEE THAT THE LORD IS GOOD!

It will change you from the inside out. You will witness a modern-day miracle, or you'll see an answered prayer. Once you recognize the change, see the miracle, or experience the answered prayer - you will taste the sweetness of God that will make you hunger for more. Your faith will multiply. You will have a supernatural strength that will carry you on to the next chapter of your life or journey. Each time I can taste the goodness of our Lord and Savior Jesus Christ, I am reminded of His love and sacrifice for me. And then I get excited to taste even more!

# WEEK 4: DAY 20
# APPLICATION

As you read these scriptures, put them into your own words in the space provided.

## PSALM 34:8

## JOHN 4:14

## ROMANS 15:13

## 1 CORINTHIANS 2:9

## EPHESIANS 3:20

## HEBREWS 4:16

Which scripture speaks the loudest to you today?

_____

_____

_____

_____

_____

_____

_____

_____

_____

_____

_____

# WEEK 5

# REVIVE -
# JEHOVAH JIREH

## SONG RECOMMENDATION FOR WORSHIP:

*"Trust in You" Lauren Daigle*

*"Oceans" by Hill Song United*

*"What a Beautiful Name," by Hillsong United*

# WEEK 5: DAY 21
# HIS PLANS ARE BIGGER

 ## ISAIAH 55:8-9 (NIV)

"For my thoughts are not your thoughts, neither are your ways my ways." declares the Lord. "As the heavens are higher than the earth, so are my ways higher than your ways and my thoughts than your thoughts."

## JEHOVAH JIREH =
## GOD IS OUR PROVIDER

Our minds cannot conceive what God knows and what He has planned for us. He's the same in the past, present, and future. I read one of A. W. Tozer's books, The Pursuit of Man, and I love this metaphor about God. I'll paraphrase it the best I can.

Look at a river and visualize yourself standing in the flowing water, headed downstream. You look behind you. You see a forceful gush of water, then quickly, it almost knocks you off your feet as it runs downstream, curving along the rocks and sediment. Imagine a river as our powerful God. The same force of water is behind us, rippling around our feet and swishing by us off into the distance. Our God is the same rushing water from our past, present and will be the same in our future.

We assume we know what we need, and nine out of ten times, we want what we can't have or don't need. Understanding that Jesus is my provider and that He's still the same powerful Jesus that performed so many miracles helped me grasp Isaiah 55:8-9. His ways are always better than mine. I remember Him taking care of me in my past that led me to where I am now; so, I have evidence in my life of His provision and constant, never changing hand.

I prayed for almost four years to get pregnant, and it felt like an eternity. Everywhere I went, pregnant bellies greeted me. They reminded me I wasn't lucky enough or good enough to become a mother. People in passing would complain about a mundane task they had to do for their kids. I will not lie; I was super sensitive, and it struck a nerve in me. I'd have killed for that problem. I felt like the odd man out. It was always on my mind, and every day felt like a slap in the face coming to terms I still wasn't pregnant. Everyone I knew had kids.

## DURING THAT WAITING PERIOD, GOD WORKED ON MY HEART.

That was the saddest and most desperate place I'd have ever been. But the Lord brought me to a place where I'd love and serve Him as my God, even if the answer was no. He brought me to a place where I'd love and serve Him as my God, even if the answer was no. Not only was it a place where God became my all, but I had to learn and accept that God knows what's best for me. Still, the feeling of wanting something so badly and realizing it may never come to pass was gut-wrenchingly painful!

During the waiting season, we are told to "Let go and let God." Still, if anyone has been in an out-of-control situation, that statement is much easier said than done. It's a daily surrender. Or better yet, it's an hourly surrender on some days. Trusting God to provide and guide us through the hard times is scary.

Looking back, I see how waiting for the Lord made everything about our journey to our little boy so much sweeter. It was the most challenging time in my life—harder than my divorce and harder than grieving the loss of my sister-in-law. I wanted to become a mother so badly. It was painful in my heart and manifested into a stomachache and piercing heartache. Daily and hourly seeking our Father was the ONLY way I survived.

# WEEK 5: DAY 21
# APPLICATION

Write these scriptures in your own words, and then reflect on prayers you've been praying and how God's way is higher than yours.

## PSALM 46:10

_____

_____

_____

_____

_____

## PSALM 37:7

_____

_____

_____

_____

_____

PSALM 62:8

_____

_____

_____

_____

_____

JEREMIAH 29:11-12

_____

_____

_____

_____

_____

# WEEK 5: DAY 22
## CROSSNG OVER

When the Israelites finally reached the Jordan River, they were too scared to cross because of the giants that stood on the other side. When our relationship with Christ is strengthened, and we genuinely want the life He has for us, He'll sanctify us. Then allows us to cross over into a deeper and more meaningful relationship with Him. This is when we graduate from a baby Christian to a mature Christian.

Maybe we're scared to go deeper into a relationship with Him. What will He expect from me? Am I good enough? What if I fail? What if this or that never changes? Will I be able to trust Him 100%?

If our hearts yearn to be molded into the likeness of Christ, then God will protect and take care of us. Reading scripture and allowing it to penetrate our hearts and mind

begins the sanctification process. He sanctifies us as we reached the Jordan. He wants us to take that leap of faith to go deeper and press forward on learning more about our Lord.

As the Israelites reach the Jordan, God had them place stones at the bank to be landmarks for generations to come to see how God led them out of Egypt and into the Promise Land. Looking back on my life, I have a few stones to mark monumental moments where I crossed into the Jordan with Christ. These are moments I'll never forget and will tell my children and grandchildren of God's goodness and grace. It's when we take that leap of faith and believe wholeheartedly that God is directing us out of something or onto a new path. We cross over and surrender and trust He's got this! That's when we put all that we've learned into practice and live out our faith.

# WEEK 5: DAY 22
# APPLICATION

Read these scriptures and answer the questions in journal form in the space provided.

 JOSHUA 4:1-24

PSALM 25:1,4-5, 8-10

HEBREWS 11:29

1 PETER 2:2-3

## DAY 22

Are you crossing over into the Jordan?

_____

_____

_____

_____

What are some of your stones that represent monumental moments of full surrender and trust in the Lord?

_____

_____

_____

What giants keep you from crossing over the Jordan River or diving all in with Christ?

_____

_____

_____

Maybe you're there and just haven't known what to do or how to cross.
Taking that leap of faith is a colossal task and takes full dependency on Christ.

_____

_____

_____

_____

# WEEK 5: DAY 23
## WALKING ON WATER WITH JESUS
## STANDING ON THE PROMISES OF GOD

# MATTHEW 14:22-33 (NIV)
## JESUS WALKS ON THE WATER

"Immediately, Jesus made the disciples get into the boat and go on ahead of him to the other side, while he dismissed the crowd. After he had dismissed them, he went up on a mountainside by himself to pray.

Later that night, he was there alone, and the boat was already a considerable distance from land, buffeted by the waves because the wind was against it. Shortly before dawn, Jesus went out to them, walking on the lake. When the disciples saw him walking on the lake, they were terrified. 'It's a ghost,' they said and cried out in fear. But Jesus immediately said to them: 'Take courage! It is I. Don't be afraid.'

'Lord, if it's you,' Peter replied, 'tell me to come to you on the water.' 'Come,' he said. Then Peter got down out of the boat, walked on the water, and came toward Jesus. But when he saw the wind, he was afraid and, beginning to sink, cried out, 'Lord, save me!' Immediately Jesus reached out his hand and caught him. 'You of little faith,' he said, 'why did you doubt?' And when they climbed into the boat, the wind died down. Then those who were in the boat worshiped him, saying, 'Truly you are the Son of God.'"

Like Peter, we must keep our eyes on Jesus. He may call us out to sea, He may allow us to get caught in a storm, or we decide without His help and end up in the deep, sinking.

However, we end up out at sea, we must learn to keep our eyes on HIM. The second we take our focus off Him, we will sink. Like we've said before, our enemy will place doubt and fear into us just like he did in Peter. It's when the rubber meets the road, and we're forced to see what we are made of.

Are we going to put our hope and faith in Jesus to get us out or help us through? Or are we going to give up and feel sorry for ourselves, isolate ourselves, and believe the lies that tell us He doesn't love us?

Whether we are out at sea or on dry land, we are all praying for God's direction and help. When we pair up our requests with scripture, we claim that promise over our lives. This was huge for me to grasp. It took the guesswork out of wondering if this was selfish of me to pray what I was asking for.

Is this even in God's will? Can I find scripture about my prayer request? Will my prayer request bring Glory to God if answered? Does God get honored through my prayer or devotion?

We can pray for God to give us scripture to claim over our family and issues we are praying about. It's then that we can stand in the Promises of the Lord and wait for the day we can proclaim, "Yes and Amen!"

# WEEK 5: DAY 23
# APPLICATION

Read this scripture and answer the questions in journal form.

 2 CORINTHIANS 1:20

LET'S KEEP OUR EYES ON JESUS AND CLAIM THE PROMISES OF THE LORD. THIS SETS US FREE!

DAY 23

What are some of your current pleads,
prayer requests this week or the last few months?

_____

_____

_____

_____

_____

_____

_____

Look up scripture for these prayers.
(Google search if you need to :) Pray, and He will reveal them to you.

_____

_____

_____

_____

_____

_____

_____

# WEEK 5: DAY 23
## DISCERNMENT

Discerning what God wants us to do and hearing His voice is essential in our mature adult walk with the Lord. When my husband Brian and I were trying to get pregnant, and it wasn't happening, my prayers shifted. One day, Lord, let us get pregnant if it's in your will. And later, Lord, should we look at infertility treatment, procedures, or adoption?

I had close friends undergoing the same struggles. They were having success with treatments and procedures, so the pressure and thoughts circled around my head for weeks. I knew that if we went forth with anything, I had to have God's blessing. I needed peace; I needed clarity if this was the route He wanted us to take! We discovered that between the both of us, the odds were against us. When they say your chances are low and ours are very low... you know it's not looking good.

Still, my doctor said it would happen when it's God's time and not to give up. Hearing him say that didn't persuade me or help me trust God any more than I already was. With our odds, I wanted to seek infertility help. So, I prayed. And quickly, God answered, "No." "Be Still."

Excuse me, do what? Be still? But something is clearly not working correctly, so how on earth will we get pregnant? During the next two years, I would hear, "Be still, my child," "Wait on me," "I got this, be still," in my heart. I would read countless scriptures of waiting and being still before the Lord. I knew that if we did infertility treatments that we'd be going against His plan for us. I knew I was hearing be still, and so Brian agreed with me we should stay still. I listened to His voice more and more. It was so soft and soothing and brought so much comfort. I would journal out my thoughts, and every time I felt the Lord telling me something, I'd back it up with scripture. I knew it

was the Holy Spirit speaking and guiding me. I played mind games with myself, trying to change my thought process, believing maybe it was my own self-consciousness. Still, every time - the same soft voice overruled every other thought. I'd pray for clarity that if this wasn't you, Father, stop it.

Scripture after scripture was brought teaching me about our helper and our counselor. As I became more familiar with His voice, His command to be still continued to grow stronger. Time was passing, yet I knew what God wanted me to do. And it was to wait on Him. He had a plan, and my timing wasn't His.

I took that huge lesson of praying for direction and discerning what He wants me to do and now apply it to all areas of life. I prayed about this very Bible study for God to guide me and show me what He wanted it to be. I pray about small and big decisions for our son, and I pray about how I should respond to things or how to pray for my husband.

Discerning the Voice of God has changed my life! I have received so much peace in return from our Lord, and He is so faithful! Not once has ever forsaken me or not held up His end of the promise!

Remember my enlightenment on Day 21. God is so faithful. After this epiphany, I had a random thought of taking a pregnancy test just to see since my cycle was late. And sure enough, two blue lines appeared! God's promises are never broken.

As you search for your own answered prayer, pray for God to speak to you, to give you a simple word or phrase. Over time, you will recognize His voice in your heart. Sometimes He'll put the thought and then confirm it through someone else, a song, or even a sermon.

# WEEK 5: DAY 24
# APPLICATION

Read these scriptures about our helper and journal what the Lord has taught you about the Holy Spirit.

## ISAIAH 9:6-7

## LUKE 3:21-22

## JOHN 16:7-15

## JOHN 20:19-31

## EPHESIANS 1:13-14, 17-21

## EPHESIANS 3:16-21

## 1 THESSALONIANS 4:7-8

# WEEK 5: DAY 25
## FOLLOW HIM, FOR HE IS FAITHFUL.

Let's look back and review what we've discussed. Remember this study and bring yourself back to the Lord when time passes and you feel distant from Him. We must be honest here; we are imperfect humans with every intention of serving the Lord with all our hearts daily until our time here is up. If we don't keep our armor on and daily seek Him, we will lose sight of Him. Our focus will be on other people and things, and before we know it, we'll be doubting His greatness.

## SO, LET'S LOOK BACK ON THE LAST FIVE WEEKS.

We learned that the time in the wilderness is necessary to teach us about God's attributes and His ways.

We understand what full dependency on Christ means, following him by the pillar at night and clouds by the day, along with trusting Christ and allowing him to be our daily bread. We have tasted and seen that the Lord is Good!!

We accepted His plans are bigger and better for us than we could ever imagine, and we took that leap of faith and crossed over into the Jordan River with Christ. We learned how to stay afloat and walk on the water with Jesus and how to discern Him and His ways.

Our God is so much bigger than we give Him credit for. As one friend said it best, "We are warring men and women of Zion!" We are mature sons and daughters of Christ. We have value and worth in Him. It's our job to fight for our loved ones and spread the Gospel to as many as we can. God answers prayers. He heals the sick and still makes modern-day miracles; we have the birthright of Christ. We cannot allow our past and failures or doubt to steal what the Lord has created for us. Our union with Him is extraordinary. We, my friends, are the chosen; called to be ambassadors for Christ! We are to BREATHE IN more of our Lord each day!

# FIRST, WE WERE HONEST

and real with God. We told Him what was keeping us from diving all in with him. We acknowledged His presence is everywhere, and He's right by our side. Then we went back to our salvation and found our identity in Christ.

# WE DISCOVERED

our Egypt's that hold us back, and we thought about all our experiences with Him that ignited His fire in our hearts.

# WE EXAMINED

our hearts and forgave those who've wronged us, and we forgave ourselves for poor decisions and mistakes.

# WE ACCEPTED

our past is part of our purpose, and He will qualify the called.

# WE LEARNED

God wants us ready to fight the spiritual war with his armor designed to keep us strong and safe.

# WE RECOGNIZED

we cannot allow our relationship with the Lord to become a checklist of dos and don'ts. Instead, we need to seek Him and allow Him to change our hearts to want to do for the Lord.

# WE IDENTIFIED

the fruits of the spirit and how they are living proof when we are walking with the Lord.

# WE RECEIVED

the power of prayer and how He wants us to pray about all things with His authority.

# WEEK 5: DAY 25
# APPLICATION

Think back over the last five weeks and share your favorite scriptures, experiences with Christ, or what you have learned.

 ## MATTHEW 7:7-8 (NIV)
## ASK, SEEK, KNOCK

"Ask, and it will be given to you; seek and you will find; knock, and the door will be opened to you. For everyone who asks receives; the one who seeks finds; and to the one who knocks, the door will be opened."

## JAMES 4:8A (NASB)
## DRAW NEAR TO GOD

"Draw near to God, and He will draw near to you,"

DAY 25

JUST BREATHE

JUST BREATHE

If you've enjoyed this study, I encourage your feedback and look forward to your review!

Post a review on AMAZON, Goodreads, and Google Books.

## CONNECT WITH ME ON SOCIAL MEDIA

 Instagram: @andreapbourgeois

 Facebook: @andreapbourgeoisblog

 Website: andreapbourgeois.com

JUST BREATHE

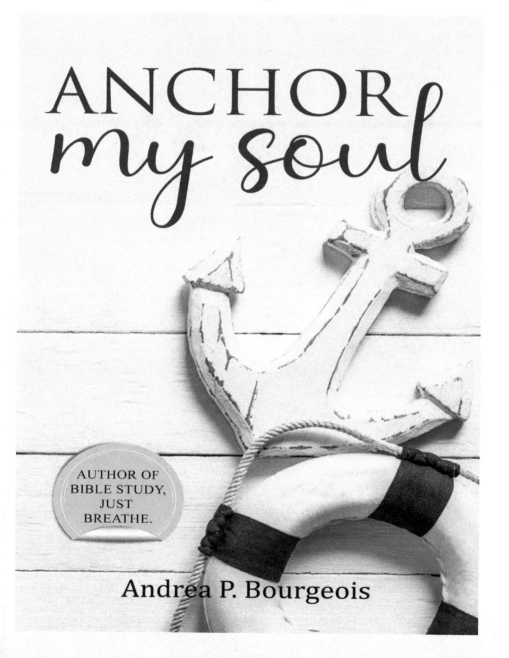

# ANCHOR
## my soul

AUTHOR OF
BIBLE STUDY,
JUST
BREATHE.

Andrea P. Bourgeois